SPOOKTACULAR

JOKES
RIDDLES AND

for Kids Ages 8-12

Edited by Emily McKeon

SPOOKTACULAR JOKES AND RIDDLES FOR AGES 8-12

Spot illustrations: Creative Fabrica & Freepik.com

CONTENTS

INTRODUCTION

Do you love the spine-tingling spirit of Halloween? Then this is the book for you! Jam packed with over 250 spooky jokes about ghosts, vampires, witches, and monsters, it's sure to deliver hours of laughs and frights for the whole family.

Whether you're reading alone, or with others, these laugh-out-loud jokes are simply eerie-sistible!

Who said Halloween has to be all scary?

1

GHOST JOKES

What's a ghost's favorite play?

Romeo and Ghoul-iet.

What does a ghost mom say when she gets in the car?

Fasten your sheet-belts.

What room does a ghost not need in a house?

A living room.

How do ghosts send letters?

Through the ghost office.

Why do ghosts like to ride in elevators?

It raises their spirits.

What kind of key does a ghost use to unlock a door?

A SPOO-key!

What did the mommy ghost say to the noisy young ghost who kept interrupting?

"Spook when you're spooken to."

Where does a ghost go on vacation?

Mali-boo.

Where does a ghost go on vacation?

What do ghosts use to wash their hair?

Sham-boo.

Knock, Knock!

Who's there?

Boo!

Boo who?

Don't cry, it's only a knock-knock joke.

What happens when a ghost gets lost in the fog?

He is mist.

Where do toddler ghosts stay when their parents are at work?

Day scare!

How can you tell if a ghost is scared?

He's white as a sheet.

What is a ghost's favorite position to play in hockey?

Ghoulie.

What is in a ghost's nose?

Boo-gers.

What should you say if you meet a ghost?

"How do you boo?"

What sort of birthday cake do ghosts prefer?

I scream cake.

What do ghosts put on their turkey?

Grave-y.

What is a baby ghost's favorite game to play on Halloween?

Peek-a-boo.

Where do ghosts buy their Halloween candy?

At the ghost-ery store!

What do ghosts give out to trick or treaters?

Boo-berries.

Which type of pants do ghosts wear?

Boo jeans!

Knock, Knock!

Who's there?

Ghost.

Ghost who?

Ghost stand over there and I'll bring you some candy!

What is a ghost's favorite kind of drink?

Ghoul-aid.

What kind of horse do ghosts ride?

A night-mare

What kind of cereal does a ghost have for breakfast?

Rice Creepies.

What do ghosts eat for dinner?

Spook-ghetti!

💀

What does a ghost call a mistake?

A boo-boo.

🌙

Why did the ghost cancel his comedy show?

He didn't want to get booed.

Why did the baby ghost cry?

He missed his mummy.

What did the boy ghost say to the girl ghost?

"You sure are boo-tiful!"

On which day are ghosts most scary?

Fright-day!

Knock, Knock!

Who's there?

Ice Cream.

Ice cream who?

Ice cream every time I see a ghost!

Why do ghosts love going to amusement parks?

Because they can ride lots of roller-GHOST-ers.

What did one ghost say to the other ghost?

"Do you believe in people?"

What is a ghost's favorite bedtime story?

Little Boo Peep.

What do baby ghosts wear on their little feet?

Boo-ties!

Where do fashionable ghosts shop?

Boo-tiques.

Who did the scary ghost invite to his party?

Any old friend he could dig up.

Knock, Knock!

Who's there?

Zoom.

Zoom who?

Zoom did you think I was, a real ghost?

What does a panda ghost eat?

Bam-BOO.

Why did the ghost quit studying?

Because he was too ghoul for school.

Why do ghosts make the best cheerleaders?

Because they have spirit.

**What do you call a
ghost in the middle
of the ocean?**

A boo-y.

**Where does a baby
ghost sit in the car?**

A boo-ster seat.

**Why do demons and
ghouls hang out
together?**

Because demons are a
ghoul's best friend!

2
WITCH
JOKES

What was the witch's favorite subject in school?

Spelling.

What do you call two witches who live together?

Broom-mates!

What's the problem with twin witches?

You never know which witch is which.

What do witches ask for at hotels?

Broom service.

💀

How do you turn off the lights on Halloween?

Use the light s-witch.

🌙

Why was the witch's broom late?

It over-swept.

What happens to witches who break the school rules?

They get ex-spelled.

What do witches put on their bagels?

Scream cheese.

What made the witch go to the hospital?

She had a dizzy spell.

Knock, Knock.

Who's there?

Witch.

Witch who?

Witch one of you can fix my broomstick?

What do witches put on to go trick-or-treating?

Mas-scare-a.

What do you call a witch who lives at the beach?

A sand-witch.

What do witches put in their hair?

Scare spray.

What noise does a witch's breakfast cereal make?

Snap, cackle and pop!

Why shouldn't an angry witch take her broom trick or treating?

She might fly off the handle.

What do witches race on?

Vroomsticks!

**What do you call a
witch's garage?**

A broom closet.

**How do you make a
witch itch?**

Take away the W.

**What game do witches
play on Halloween?**

Hide-and-ghost-seek!

What did the witch say to her victim while she was waiting?

Bewitcha in a minute!

Why do witches only fly on brooms?

Vacuum cleaners are too heavy.

How does a witch tell the time?

She looks at her witch-watch!

3
DRACULA
JOKES

Why did Dracula take cold medicine?

Because he was coffin too much.

How does Dracula stay fit?

He plays bat-minton!

Who did Dracula go on a date with?

His ghoul-friend!

What is Dracula's favorite cake flavor?

Vein-ella.

What did Dracula say about his wife?

It was love at first bite.

Which Halloween monster is good at math?

Count Dracula.

Where does Dracula keep his money?

At the blood bank.

Why couldn't Dracula make a pancake?

Because he messed up the bat-ter every time.

Why can't Dracula play baseball?

He lost his bat.

Who gives Dracula the most candy on Halloween?

His fang-club.

How do vampires start their letters?

Tomb it may concern.

What would be the national holiday for a nation of vampires?

Fangs-giving!

Knock, knock.

Who's there?

Ivana.

Ivana who?

Ivana suck your blood!

Why do vampires have a hard time making friends?

Because they are a pain in the neck.

How do vampires get around on Halloween?

On blood vessels.

What's it called when a vampire has trouble with his house?

A grave problem.

Why are vampires bad at art?

They are only able to draw blood.

Why do people like vampires so much?

Because they are FANG-tastic.

Why did the vampire need mouthwash?

Because he had bat breath.

Knock, Knock!

Who's there?

Tyson.

Tyson who?

Tyson garlic around your neck to keep the vampires away.

What is a vampire's favorite fruit?

A blood orange.

☾

What's a vampire's favorite fruit?

Neck-tarine.

What happens to a vampire in the snow?

Frostbite.

What type of coffee does a vampire drink?

De-coffin-ated.

What do you give a vampire when he's sick?

Coffin-drops.

What would you get if you crossed a vampire and a teacher?

Lots of blood tests!

How can you tell when a vampire has been in a bakery?

All the jelly has been sucked out of the jelly doughnuts.

Why did the vampire keep acting all batty?

It was in his blood.

What's a vampire's worst fear?

Tooth decay!

Why did the vampire break up with his girlfriend?

Because she wasn't his blood type.

(

What did the polite vampire say?

Fang you very much!

What do you call a vampire with asthma?

Vlad the Inhaler

4

MUMMY

JOKES

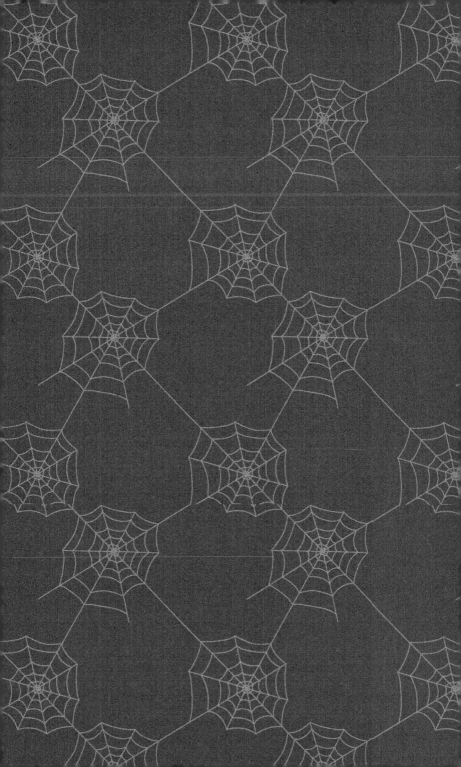

Why don't mummies have friends?

Because they're too wrapped up in themselves.

Why don't mummies take time off?

They're afraid to unwind.

How do mummies tell their future?

They read their horror-scope.

What genre of music does a mummy like the best?

Wrap!

Why couldn't the mummy go to school with the witch?

He couldn't spell.

Who does the mummy go to for moral support?

To his mummy.

What is the best job for a mummy during holidays?

A gift wrapper.

Did you hear about the scary couple at prom this year?

It was a mummy and his ghoul-friend.

Where do mummies go for a swim?

To the Dead Sea.

Knock, Knock.

Who's there?

Mum.

Mum who?

Mummy, that's who!

5

ZOMBIE
JOKES

What is white, black and dead all over?

A zombie trick-or-treating in a tuxedo.

What does a zombie call his parents?

Mummy and Deady.

What's a zombie's favorite weather?

Cloudy, with a chance of brain.

Where do zombies live?

On a dead end street.

Why do zombies never eat comedians?

They taste funny.

Why did the zombie stay home from school?

He felt rotten.

When do zombies finish trick or treating?

When they are dead tired.

What did the baby zombie want for her birthday?

A deady bear.

What do you call zombies in pajamas?

The sleepwalking dead.

What do you call a movie about zombies finding true love?

A zom-com.

What kind of bread do zombies like?

Whole brain.

What is a zombie's favorite appetizer?

Finger food!

Knock, Knock.

Who's there?

Zom.

Zom who?

Zombie-utiful day, isn't it?

What type of dogs do zombies like the most?

Bloodhounds.

What does it take to become a zombie?

Dead-ication.

Why did the zombie quit his teaching job?

He only had one pupil left.

6
SKELETON
JOKES

Why did the skeleton start a fight?

Because he had
a bone to pick.

Why was the skeleton afraid of the storm?

He didn't have any guts.

What is a skeleton's favorite musical instrument?

A trombone.

Are skeletons good at painting?

No, they prefer making skull-ptures.

How did the skeleton know it was going to rain on Halloween?

He felt it in his bones.

What did the skeleton bring to the dinner party?

Spare ribs.

Why do skeletons love to drink milk?

It's good for the bones.

9

What does the skeleton chef say when he serves you a meal?

"Bone Appetit!"

What transportation does a skeleton take?

A skelecopter.

What do you call a skeleton who lays around all day?

Lazy bones.

Why don't skeletons like Halloween candy?

They don't have the stomach for it.

What does a skeleton wear for Halloween?

A cos-tomb.

Why did the skeleton climb up the tree?

Because a dog was after his bones.

What do you call a cleaning skeleton?

The Grim Sweeper.

Do you know any skeleton jokes?

Yes, but you wouldn't find them very humerus.

Knock, Knock!

Who's there?

Bone.

Bone who?

Bone appetit, it's time for candy!

Why do skeletons have low self-esteem?

They have no body to love.

What does a French skeleton say?

Bone Jour!

Who won the skeleton beauty contest?

No body.

7

FRANKENSTEIN

JOKES

What kind of Frankenstein loves to disco?

The boogieman.

☠

Where does Frankenstein go shopping for new parts?

The gross-ery store

☾

What game does Frankenstein play?

Hide and shriek!

How does Frankenstein like his eggs?

Terror-fried.

What kind of car does Frankenstein drive on Halloween night?

A monster truck.

What is a Frankenstein's favorite cheese?

Munster.

Who does Frankenstein buy his cookies from?

Ghoul scouts.

What did Frankenstein say after being struck by lightning?

I needed that.

What monster plays tricks on Halloween?

Prank-enstein.

Knock, Knock!

Who's there?

Ooze.

Ooze who?

Ooze that monster over there?

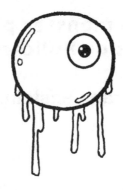

What does Frankenstein put in his chili?

Human bean-ings.

How does Frankenstein like his coffee?

Scream and sugar.

What does Frankenstein turn on in the summertime?

The scare conditioner.

**What do you call a
Frankenstein who is really
bad at scaring people?**

A Halloweenie!

**What is it called when
Frankenstein takes
control of your airplane?**

A terror-flying experience!

**What should you say when
you bump into an angry
Frankenstein monster?**

Bye, bye!

Knock, Knock!

Who's there?

Frank!

Frank who?

Frankenstein.

Why was Frankenstein going to a psychiatrist?

One of his screws was loose.

How can you stop Frankenstein from charging?

Take away his credit card.

What kind of dog did Frankenstein want for Christmas?

A Lab.

8

SCARECROW

JOKES

Why didn't the scarecrow eat dinner?

He was already stuffed.

How does the scarecrow like to drink his milk?

With a straw.

What is a scarecrow's favorite fruit?

A straw-berry.

Why did the scarecrow get a promotion?

He was out standing in his field.

How do scarecrows say hello?

'Hay!'

Why didn't the scarecrow like standing in the radish field?

He got beet up!

9

WEREWOLF
JOKES

What do you call a werewolf with no legs?

Anything you like – he can't chase you.

What do you call a sleeping werewolf?

An unaware-wolf.

Why do werewolves howl at the moon?

Because no one else will do it for them.

When do werewolves go trick or treating?

Howl-o-ween.

What did the werewolf eat after getting his teeth cleaned?

The dentist.

What's a werewolf's favorite day of the week?

Moon-day.

**What do you call a
werewolf with a fever?**

A hot dog.

**What happened when
the werewolf
swallowed a clock?**

He got ticks.

**How do werewolves
eat lunch?**

They wolf it down.

What do you call a werewolf that can't decide what to wear?

A what to wear-wolf.

What did the cowboy say when the werewolf ate his dog?

"Well, doggone!"

Why was the werewolf arrested at the butcher's shop?

He was caught chop-lifting.

Knock, Knock.

Who's there?

Howl.

Howl who?

Howl you dress for Halloween this year?

Where are werewolf movies made?

Howl-lywood.

What do you call a werewolf escapologist?

Hairy Houdini.

Why did the poor werewolf chase his own tail?

He was trying to make ends meet.

Where do werewolves hate shopping?

The flea market.

How do you make a werewolf laugh?

Give it a funny bone.

What do you call a really cold, young werewolf?

A pup-sicle.

Did you hear about the comedian who entertained at a werewolves' party?

He had them howling all night.

What do you call a werewolf who works as a lumberjack?

A Timber Wolf.

What did the Uber driver say to the werewolf?

"Where, wolf?"

10
OTHER
CREEPERS

What do dentists hand out at Halloween?

Candy. It's good for business.

What kind of TV do you find in a haunted house?

Wide-scream.

What do birds give to trick or treaters?

Tweets.

Knock, Knock!

Who's there?

Spell.

Spell who?

Okay, W-H-O.

**What Halloween candy
is never on time
for the party?**

Choco-LATE.

**How do you mend
a jack-o'-lantern?**

With a pumpkin patch.

**Why was all of the food
gone at the end of the
Halloween party?**

Everyone was a goblin.

Why was the candy corn booed off the stage?

All of his jokes were too corny!

What do you call two spiders that were just married?

Newly-webbed.

Why are graveyards so noisy?

Because of all the coffin!

Why are spiders great baseball players?

They know how
to catch flies!

What do birds say on Halloween?

"Trick or Tweet!"

Why was the cemetery chosen to be the perfect location to write a movie?

Because it had great plots.

Knock, knock.

Who's there?

Dishes.

Dishes who?

Dishes a very scary haunted house!

What does an evil hen lay?

Deviled eggs.

What do you call a field full of eyeballs?

An eye patch.

When is it bad luck to be followed by a black cat?

If you are a mouse.

**What has hundreds
of ears but can't
hear a thing?**

A cornfield.

**Why did the headless
horseman go into
business?**

He wanted to get
a head in life.

**What's a ghoul's
favorite bean?**

A human bean.

What treat do eye doctors give out on Halloween?

Candy corneas.

Who helped the little pumpkin cross the road?

The crossing gourd.

What do you call a black cat that was caught by the police?

The purr-patrator.

FUNNY PUNS

Slipped on a pumpkin today. It caught me off gourd.

* * *

Don't go goblin up all my candy.

* * *

I only have pumpkin pies for you.

Witching you a
Happy Halloween!

* * *

Your costume is so realistic
that it's un-candy!

* * *

Halloween is going to be
great. I can feel it
in my bones!

* * *

Eat, drink, and be scary!

* * *

Vampires hate peaches,
but they love
neck-tarines.

THANK YOU!

Thank you for your purchase. If you enjoyed this book, please consider dropping us a review by scanning the QR code below. It takes only 5 seconds and helps small independent publishers like us.

Made in the USA
Monee, IL
25 October 2022